Little Books of Guidance
Finding answers to life's big questions!

Also in the series:

T0272770

THE WAY OF LOVE

Learn

A little
book of
guidance

CHURCH
PUBLISHING
INCORPORATED

Unless otherwise noted, the Scripture quotations contained herein are from the New Revised Standard Version Bible, copyright © 1989 by the Division of Christian Education of the National Council of Churches of Christ in the U.S.A. Used by permission. All rights reserved.

Scripture quotations marked (NIV) are taken from the Holy Bible, New International Version®, NIV®. Copyright © 1973, 1978, 1984, 2011 by Biblica, Inc.™ Used by permission of Zondervan. All rights reserved worldwide. www.zondervan.com The "NIV" and "New International Version" are trademarks registered in the United States Patent and Trademark Office by Biblica, Inc.™

This book compiles text from the following sources:
Margaret Guenther, *At Home in the World: A Rule of Life for the Rest of Us* (New York: Seabury, 2006); Vicki K. Black and Peter W. Wenner, *Welcome to the Bible* (Harrisburg PA: Morehouse Press, 2007); Julia Gatta, *Life in Christ: Practicing Christian Spirituality* (New York: Church Publishing, 2018); *The Art of Transformation: Three Things that Churches Do that Change Everything* (New York: Church Publishing, 2017)

Church Publishing
19 East 34th Street
New York, NY 10016
www.churchpublishing.org

Cover design by Jennifer Kopec, 2Pug Design
Typeset by Denise Hoff

A record of this book is available from the Library of Congress.

ISBN-13: 978-1-64065-170-8 (pbk.)
ISBN-13: 978-1-64065-171-5 (ebook)

Contents

Introduction

I pray that you, being rooted and established in love, may have power, together with all the Lord's holy people, to grasp how wide and long and high and deep is the love of Christ, and to know this love that surpasses knowledge—that you may be filled to the measure of all the fullness of God.

—Ephesians 3:17-19, NIV

At the 79th General Convention of the Episcopal Church in July 2018, Presiding Bishop Michael B. Curry called the Church to practice *The Way of Love*. This is an invitation to all of us, young and old alike, to "grow more deeply with Jesus Christ at the center of our lives, so we can bear witness to his way of love in and for the world."

With this call, Bishop Curry named seven practices that can help us grow deeper in our relationship with God, Jesus, and our neighbors as we also learn how to live into our baptismal promises more fully. In today's world of busy schedules, hurried meals, and twenty-four-hour news cycles, it is now more imperative that we make and take the time to center ourselves and follow the way of Jesus. This might mean revisioning and reshaping the pattern and rhythm of our daily life—finding a slice of time to center our thoughts on Jesus. Within these pages you will find ideas to engage in the practice of learn as you walk on *The Way of Love: Practices for a Jesus-Centered Life*.

To be a Christian is to be a seeker. We seek love: to know God's love, to love, and to be loved by others. It also means learning to love ourselves as a child of God. We seek freedom from the many forces that pull us from living as God created us to be: sin, fear, oppression, and division. God desires us to be dignified, whole, and free. We also seek abundant life. This is a life that is overflowing with joy, peace, generosity, and delight. It is a life where there is enough for all because we share with abandon. We seek a life of meaning, giving back to God and living for others and not just for ourselves. Ultimately we seek Jesus. Jesus is the way of love and that has the power to change lives and change the world.

How are we called to practice the Way of Love? Bishop Curry has named seven practices to follow. Like a "Rule of Life" practiced by Christians for almost two thousand years, these are ways that help us live intentionally in our daily life, following our deepest values. These are not add-ons to our day, but ways to recognize God working in us and through us.

Jesus teaches us to come before God with humble hearts, boldly offering our thanksgivings and concerns to God or simply listening for God's voice in our lives and in the world. Whether in thought, word, or deed, individually or corporately, when we pray we invite and dwell in God's loving presence. Jesus often removed himself from the crowds to quiet himself and commune with God. He gave us examples of how to pray, including the Lord's Prayer. "Will you continue in the prayers?" "I will with God's help."

Practices are challenging and can be difficult to sustain. Even though we might practice "solo" (e.g., prayer), each practice belongs to the community as a whole in which you inhabit as a whole—your family, church, or group of friends. Join with some trustworthy companions with whom to grow into this way of life; sharing and accountability help keep us grounded and steady in our practices.

This series of seven Little Books of Guidance is designed for you to discover how following certain practices can help you follow Jesus more fully in your daily life. You may already keep a spiritual discipline of praying at meals or before bed, regularly reading from the Bible, or engaging in acts of kindness toward others. If so, build upon what we offer here; if not, we offer a way to begin. Select one of the practices that interests you or that is especially important for you at this time. Watch for signs in your daily life pointing you toward a particular practice. Listen for a call from God telling you how to move closer. Anywhere is a good place to start. This is your invitation to commit to the practices of **Turn—Learn—Pray—Worship—Bless—Go—Rest**. There is no rush, each day is a new beginning. Follow Bishop Curry's call to grow in faith "following the loving, liberating, life-giving way of Jesus. His way has the power to change each of our lives and to change this world."

1 ■ Lifelong Learning and Our Life of Faith

First of all, we have to realize that learning is more than piling up books, calculating the tens of thousands of pages we have read, and accumulating data. I regret that a prayer for the gifts of the Holy Spirit, which is said over the newly baptized and after that forgotten about, is not imprinted more deeply on our consciousness:

> Sustain them, O Lord, in your Holy Spirit. Give them an inquiring and discerning heart, the courage to will and to persevere, a spirit to know and to love you, and the gift of joy and wonder in all your works. (BCP, 308)

Although we share our opposable thumbs with other primates, our inquiring minds and discerning hearts, accompanied by the tools of language and memory, are part of what it means to be made in the image of God.

We are expected to use these gifts in the service of God, to know and to love God, and in our own growth and development, to know and to love ourselves. It is temptingly easy, however, to turn off our minds and disconnect our good sense when we move from workaday to spiritual concerns. It is tempting to remain stuck in childish understandings of God and immature theological beliefs, and to feel that the work of learning is done once we have graduated from confirmation class, if we ever went at all. How easy it is to shrink from risk, to let our hearts and minds grow small and constricted instead of bold and expansive. People of faith who are well informed about economics, philosophy, political affairs, and the arts and sciences can be all too willing to turn their minds off when their faith is involved. Perhaps we fear that our feeble construct of God cannot bear the impact of critical thinking.

But Benedict, unlike his holy forebears of the desert, reminds us that any split between mind and soul is a false dichotomy; our intellects are an integral part of our spirituality. As such, they deserve a share of our time and our energy long after we have completed our formal education. "Idleness," he tells us, "is the enemy of the soul. Therefore, the brethren should be occupied at certain times with manual labor, and again at fixed hours in sacred reading" (ch. 48). Most of our labor nowadays isn't manual, but we are still a work-obsessed people. Study, however, is another matter: we live in the mistaken belief that it is the province of the young.

I was home-schooled for a year, long before the term was ever coined. My mother had no training as a teacher, but I was so eager to learn that we figured it out as we went along. Reading simply happened—we had my brother's old books, which I read to her while she worked her way through a pile of ironing. From a kindergarten teacher friend, she hit on the idea of printing one word on a 3 x 5 card, which turned into a lot of words on a great pile of cards. From these I would make stories on the floor, starting in the living room, running through the dining room and ending in the little sewing room, where I would run out of space and cards. For writing, I was allowed to use the family typewriter. It was one of the first hardships of my young life when I learned that I would have to know at least how to print my letters with a pencil.

Real school was another story. When I entered second grade after reluctantly demonstrating my prowess with a Number 2 pencil, our chief task in arithmetic was to master what the teacher called "combinations"—one plus one equals two, one plus two equals three, and so on up to ten plus ten equals twenty. We were expected to write the series of little sums over and over, acres of them, until they were permanently etched in our brains. I wonder if my present mathematical disability might have been avoided if somehow I had been made aware of the mystery and promise of numbers, a gift that had come to me naturally with words. At any rate, there was little joy and wonder as I filled page after page with ones and twos. Of course, we need to learn the basics, which are not always interesting and whose usefulness must be taken on faith. This is especially true when our faith demands that we learn to think theologically. This may send us into a kind of panic—even as we yearn to learn more and more about our faith, we may despair of our ability to contort our brains into new possibilities. Learning to think theologically is different from the learning required to gain moderate proficiency in a new language, which many of us have already managed to do adequately, if not brilliantly. Theology affects our deepest thoughts and yearnings, and we may fear that our very identity might be called into question if we delve too deeply in learning about our faith. Now I realize that *all* our serious thinking should be theological, because all knowledge is part of the mind of the God who created all that is. Even if we are unable to skate comfortably amid words like *epistemology* and *soteriology,* to say nothing of *hermeneutic,* we are all capable of learning more about our faith in God. Although useful, the arcane vocabulary can be a smoke screen, and it is reassuring to remember that Jesus's vocabulary was straightforward and deceptively simple.

God's Curriculum

So what do we study? If our aim is to apply our inquiring minds and discerning hearts to all God's works, the curriculum is vast. The book of nature is all around us. Here there can be no end to our learning, whether we are fascinated by the blight on the backyard rose bushes or the currents of the tsunami, the circulation of our blood or the exploration of space. The study of all the sciences is ultimately theological study, whether we are amateur or professional. And amateur status is not to be discounted, since the amateur is a lover who learns for the love of learning.

A fascination with words has dominated my own life of study. I still remember my excitement in my ninth-grade Latin class, which was my first encounter with a foreign language, other than bits of German learned from my father. The laborious translations and rote memorization should have been tedious, but I was enthralled by the prospect of learning unfamiliar words for such familiar things. At about the same time, I fell in love with my native English and was obnoxious in my zeal to weave my new discoveries into my homework. I still recall my satisfaction when I could finally fit "unambiguously" into a book report!

And, of course, words knit together made stories. Although I could not have articulated it when I was young, I perceived everything as a story, as narrative. Not only literature, but history, psychology, and—to my delight and surprise—even theology could be seen as part of a story. It is no accident that Jesus is Logos, the Word, and that the Bible is our big family storybook. Every now and then, if someone calls me a "theologian," I wince and try to clarify: "No, I just like stories. I like to pick words apart and push them back to their beginnings, then see how they all come together again." As I reflect now, there has been a graced coherence in my lifetime of learning: eventually everything comes together, like pieces of an intricate mosaic that will never be quite finished. This is indeed the work of a lifetime.

Abba Macarius instructed Abba Pherme to dispose of his books. He had only three, yet that was apparently enough to distract **him** from his life of prayer. By contrast, we have an abundance of avenues to learning: books, journals, film, lectures, tapes, and CD-ROMs— not to mention our eyes and ears. Augustine, Benedict, and our other monastic ancestors who valued learning lived before the information explosion. There could be no danger of excess or superficiality in their way of study. A monk read slowly and ruminated on what was read; then he probably went back and read it again. And again. It can be no accident that this very agricultural verb is used to describe monastic study: like meditative cows slowly chewing and chewing until they have got the last bit of nourishment from their mouthful of grass, the ruminant reader is in no hurry. That is how I read stories and was read to as a child, no doubt because children back then were not inundated with books. The faithful few on my shelf became old friends, to be visited regularly until I knew them by memory.

This practice proved to be useful when, as an adult, I needed to teach myself Spanish. I was not aiming for elegance or eloquence, just enough for survival. I had studied grammar diligently, but now the enterprise needed to be brought to life. I was overjoyed when I found a paperback translation of Louisa May Alcott's *Little Women* on a Mexico City pushcart. I knew then that I had found my way home on the very first page: *"Es muy triste decirlo, pero somos pobres,' mumuro Meg."* ("'It's so dreadful to be poor,' sighed Meg.") I had read, marked, learned, and inwardly digested *Little Women* when I was seven years old with a thoroughness that would have made Benedict proud. I moved triumphantly through *Mujercitas,* then returned to my pushcart source and picked up *Anne of Green Gables—Ana de los Tejados Verdes*—followed by *Las Aventuras de Sherlock Holmes.* By the time I had gone through my new little library at least twice, I could carry on comfortable if untidy conversations in my new language.

At the time I didn't assign a deeper significance to those weeks of reading; I simply saw my method as a rather pleasurable and effective means to an end. Upon reflection, however, I realized that I had so immersed myself in my childhood favorites that the words and sentences were almost a part of me. Now I was seeing them with new eyes; they had lost nothing, indeed had taken on a new texture. Gradually it has occurred to me that over the years I have read Scripture in the same way—sometimes in German or Spanish, just for the linguistic adventure—sometimes in the King James Version of the Bible of my childhood, most often nowadays in the New Revised Standard Version. We do not gallop through the sixty-six books of Holy Writ (not counting the Apocrypha) with the sense of instant mastery: "Great! Now I've done it! Now I can get on to something else." No, our engagement with Scripture is another work of a lifetime: we immerse ourselves, let ourselves sink deeper and deeper through layers of meaning, let the words become almost a part of our own skin.

There is so much to learn, and just to keep abreast of current events is an impossible task, even when we fall back on the quick fix of television news or magazine reporting. There is so much to know and to begin to understand that our brains are reeling. Yet the kind of study that Benedict prescribes demands that we apply our minds as well as our emotions to our relationship not only with God, but all that God has made. At times I am tempted to turn off my thought processes, to persuade myself that trying to understand what is happening in the Middle East and Korea, South Africa, and our inner cities, the Amazon rain forest, and the pharmaceutical industry has nothing to do with my identity in Christ. Life would be easier if empathy with human and environmental distress were sufficient, but it's not. Action is required.

Perhaps even more important is the application of our intellect to our faith. It may be disturbing to bring a certain rigor and discipline to the study of Scripture, to wrestle with its inconsistencies and let our old certainties be challenged. The good news here is that God is strong enough to withstand our poking and prodding, maybe even delights in it as a loving parent enjoys being poked and prodded by that inquisitive toddler who likes to push buttons. An unexamined faith is a dangerous faith: false gods are all around us, alive and alluring. When we think that we have God all figured out and that we are infallible interpreters of God's will, we are in trouble.

If we live by a rule, the commitment to learning should be almost as important a part of our regimen as our commitment to prayer. It keeps us from remaining at a comfortable and undemanding level of spiritual immaturity. So we keep on learning—from books, from tradition, from the shared wisdom of our community, and from our own experience. If we wish to deepen our understanding of our faith, there are so many options today: participating in an Education for Ministry (EFM) group or a class in our parish, finding a course at a local seminary or college, exploring online opportunities, or the good old-fashioned tried-and-true approach of thoughtful reading on our own. Above all, we must not be afraid to grapple with hard questions or to confront our uncertainties. The study of Scripture, theology, and church history is a rich feast to be embraced and enjoyed. Just as an unexamined life is not worth living, so an unexamined faith is not worth having.

2 ■ Learning from the Bible

One of the most difficult habits to unlearn when we approach the Bible again as adults is our relentless effort to search for *the* right answer. As young children we enjoyed our ability to imagine multiple truths in a single world: stories and myths and the things of the spirit were all intertwined with the physical reality of our everyday lives. For most of us, however, as we moved through years of schooling and took hundreds of tests for correct answers, the assumption that there is a single "right" answer to most questions became normative.

So when we come to the Bible as adults, perhaps after we have been away from church and Bible study for some time, we often bring with us the assumption that there is, somewhere, a single, "right" interpretation to the words of Scripture, and therefore the task of Bible study is to find it. Even if we did not have any exposure to the Bible in our childhood, we have certainly been exposed to this idea that the Bible is a book of God's answers to life's questions. It is disconcerting, then, to find that among all the different churches and religious traditions, there are widely differing interpretations of the same Bible verses. Furthermore, as we attend the worship services and participate in the life of a particular congregation, we discover that even within the same denomination or congregation, individual Christians can hold radically different understandings of what the Bible says. When Bible study classes deteriorate into arguments about who is right and who is wrong, tensions arise and people feel alienated from one another. Clearly, if the purpose of Bible study is to find a right interpretation of God's word we can all agree on, then the church has failed, since agreement in the church is a very rare thing.

If, on the other hand, the purpose of Bible study is something rather different, then we can let go of the need to settle on a single, correct interpretation, and instead embark on the journey of discovering what the Bible has to say about who God is, and who we are in relationship with God. It will not always be an easy journey: we will be challenged to stretch and perhaps to let go of long-held beliefs and unreflective ways of thinking, as we grow in our knowledge of God and what it means to be fully human, formed in God's image. We will not always find our companions on this journey pleasant or congenial, and we will sometimes fail to be generous with those whom we dislike or with whom we disagree. But the Bible is large enough to encompass us all.

As we have discussed elsewhere in this book, there are myriad ways to read the Bible, each with distinctive strengths and weaknesses. Sometimes we need the support and encouragement of studying the Bible with others; at other times reading alone at our own pace is more helpful. During difficult moments in our lives, the familiar and beloved passages of Scripture, especially the Psalms, can be a source of consolation and spiritual comfort. In our more focused times, undertaking the serious study of a book or theme in the Bible can be an intellectual challenge that invigorates and deepens our faith. No single approach will suffice: we need to vary the methods we use in order to see, as Ephrem the Syrian put it, the many different "facets of God's word."

In this chapter we will explore only a few of the methods for reading and studying the Bible that many people of faith have found useful over the centuries. This selection is by no means exhaustive, and we encourage you also to read the many fine books that are available today describing other approaches to the study of Scripture.

Daily Offices

If you would like to develop a broad understanding of both the Hebrew and Christian Scriptures while deepening your life of prayer, you can hardly find a better pattern to follow than using one of the lectionaries of the church. Christians have long followed the practice of hearing their Scriptures read aloud in worship and at those times in which members of the community have gathered for prayer. In the early church the readings were taken from the Hebrew Scriptures and the letters and teachings of the apostles, some of which eventually became our New Testament.

As the church evolved over the centuries, and especially in the monastic orders who kept the hours of prayer throughout the day, a "schedule" of these readings was developed to encourage communities to read the entire spectrum of books of Scripture, not just their favorite few, and to emphasize the unity of the Christian church as the faithful from many diverse places and communities gathered to read the same lessons on the same day. These daily office lectionaries were the foundation of the services of prayer throughout the day offered by the monastic communities of the Middle Ages and continue to be a valuable resource for all Christians who pray some form of the daily offices today.

In the 1979 Episcopal Book of Common Prayer, we have readings for daily prayer arranged in a Daily Office Lectionary (BCP 933–1001). While the lectionary is designed to be used primarily in the context of the offices of Morning and Evening Prayer found in the Prayer Book, the readings can also be followed on their own or in the context of other forms of daily prayer, such as the various monastic offices or books of hours that are in print today. The *Daily Office Book* (with readings in the Revised Standard Version of the Bible) and

Contemporary Office Book (with readings in the New Revised Standard Version) are available from Church Publishing for those who like the ease and simplicity of having the offices and lessons printed in a single volume. You can, of course, use any Bible to follow the readings in the Daily Office Lectionary, though you may find it convenient to keep several bookmarks or ribbons handy, to make it easier to find the various readings day after day.

The notes concerning how to use the Daily Office Lectionary (BCP 934–935) are perhaps more detailed than most of us need for personal reading, but a few notes may be particularly helpful as you get started with using the lectionary. The first paragraph describes how to find out whether you should use the readings for Year One or Year Two: one for odd-numbered years and two for even—though the beginning of the church year in Advent makes this straightforward system a bit more confusing during the month of December! The notes that follow describe how to incorporate the three lessons provided for each day into two daily offices, or what to do if you pray only one office each day. It is also interesting to note, particularly when the lessons are being read alone at home as part of a regular time of Bible study and not in the context of corporate Morning or Evening Prayer, that "any Reading may be lengthened at discretion." In other words, if you have the time and inclination, you are quite free to read the passages before and after a particular reading—and this is often an important way of deepening your understanding of the passage given for that day. Misinterpreting a passage because we are reading snippets of the Bible out of context is one of the inherent dangers of any lectionary-based system of Bible reading, and remembering to glance at the paragraphs that precede and follow the reading is one way of lessening that risk.

The concluding paragraphs in the Daily Office Lectionary notes concern the readings from the Psalms. In this lectionary, portions of the Psalms are read in a seven-week pattern, with some interruptions for feast days in the church year. However, the Prayer Book also offers the alternative for a monthly reading of the Psalms straight through from beginning to end within the pages of the Psalter itself. You will find these thirty-day divisions printed in italics above some psalms: on the first day of the month, for example, you would read Psalms 1 through 5 in the morning and Psalms 6 through 8 in the evening (see BCP 585 and 589). You may find it helpful to try both patterns over the course of several years. While the lectionary sets forth three readings for each day, along with several psalms, you can also use the lectionary to follow one book at a time. Simply choose one of the three readings listed across the page, and follow that reading down the page, day by day. In this way, you can use this lectionary as a six-year course of studying a large portion of the Bible. As we mentioned in our discussion of the lectionary in the previous chapter, you could also use the readings of Sunday lectionary as a guide for studying the Bible in conjunction with worship, either as a group or as an individual.

Reading Through a Book of the Bible

Another approach to reading the Bible is to select a particular book and read it straight through, perhaps a chapter or two each day. This approach has much to recommend it, especially when you are interested in studying a particular book or section of the Bible (such as the Pentateuch or the letters of Paul) in some depth. Reading a book from beginning to end allows you to discover the contexts in which passages you may hear read aloud in worship are found. You also gain a sense of the distinctive "voices" of the authors of the books of the Bible: Paul's letters sound very different from the prophecies of Isaiah; the historical prose of Chronicles tells the story of Israel's relationship with God from a different perspective than the spiritual immediacy of the poetry and prayer of the Psalms; even the gospels tell the same story of the life of Jesus through distinctive voices and points of view.

Annotated study Bibles can be of significant help for this sort of reading. They usually provide an introduction to each book of the Bible that sets the book in its historical context, describe the authors or communities from which it came, and usually summarize the book's main points. Further annotations and comments within the text provide clues to the interpretations of confusing passages or words, identify sections and divisions within the book, and point the way to cross-references of other texts in the Bible that might illuminate the passage in question.

Commentaries are also valuable aids to study, though as when choosing an annotated study Bible, it is worth doing some research about the interpretive slant of the editors and authors of the commentaries you choose to read. Some, like the *New Jerome Biblical Commentary*, are bound in a single volume; most focus on a particular book or books of the Bible—the Anchor Bible series is a good example. Church libraries often have a selection of biblical commentaries to borrow, and having two or even three at hand while you are reading can help balance and inform different interpretations. They range in difficulty from the extremely detailed and learned to the more accessible, so take the time to choose wisely according to what your particular needs are.

It is also helpful to have several translations handy, for as we discussed earlier, each translation of the Bible is in a very real sense an interpretation of the text from a particular perspective. For those who have an interest in biblical Hebrew and Greek, learning enough of those languages to read the books of the Bible in their original language can provide profound insights into the meanings intended by the authors. Even gaining a simple grasp of important vocabulary within a passage can alter the meaning significantly.

Consider the story at the end of John's gospel, for example, in which the risen Jesus appears to Simon Peter and asks him three times, "Do you love me?" Peter replies yes each time, and we might wonder why Jesus felt the need to ask him three times. Perhaps it is simply a way of letting Peter know that his three denials have been forgiven, as would seem the most obvious interpretation. Yet by using an interlinear Greek-English New Testament, we can see that the Greek word for "love" used in the story changes: the word in Jesus's first two questions is *agapé*, the unconditional love of God. Peter, however, responds with the Greek word for the profound love of human friendship, *phileo*. In Jesus's third question he follows Peter's use of *phileo*, and John notes that "Peter felt hurt" that Jesus had asked him in this way. He replies, "Lord, you know everything; you know that I love [*phileo*] you." It would be an interesting study to follow this intriguing clue further by understanding more about the different Greek and Hebrew words translated as "love" in English Bibles. A commentary that includes references to the Greek New Testament or Hebrew Scriptures would be useful in this sort of word study.

Group Study

The convenience of studying the Bible individually at home makes it an attractive way of coming to the Bible as an adult. But most people find it very difficult to develop the discipline necessary to do more serious studies on their own. To gain a deeper connection to God and God's story in the Bible requires regularity and persistence. The Bible is a big book. As the lectionaries indicate, even doing three short readings each day of the year, it takes two years to read most of the Bible—or six years if we read only one passage a day. To nurture a growing relationship with God and God's word will require some consistent work. While some people are able to develop this discipline by themselves, most of us need others to support us, encourage us, and hold us accountable.

It is no accident that the readings assigned in lectionaries were intended to be read in public liturgies. The church long ago discovered that people needed the discipline of joining with others at a specific time and place if they were going to go further in their spiritual journeys with God and God's word. If your church has a daily service of Morning or Evening Prayer, participating in these services regularly can be a good way to develop the practice of making daily connections with the Bible.

A Bible study group can also be a community in which you read the Bible regularly. Many Bible study groups meet weekly or in some other regular pattern, though members of the group might be asked to read the materials to be studied on a daily basis. By being a part of a group of people who are all reading the same material, you gain several advantages. First, you have a weekly reason to do the assigned reading. Even if you are unable to find time daily to read, you should be able to find some time during the week to read the assigned lessons. Second, you have others with whom to discuss the passages. Some of the group may be more familiar with the Bible and can help to explain parts that are difficult, and often a leader will do some research to help the group deepen its understanding. At a minimum, you will have other people of faith who are likewise seeking to know and understand how God is speaking to them in these passages. Third, you have a chance not only to read, but also to *hear* the passages. The practice of silently reading the words of the Bible on a printed page is a relatively recent phenomenon; for centuries the Bible was most often heard aloud in the community of the faithful, who listened together for what God might be saying to them through the Scriptures. It is amazing how just hearing a passage can awaken all kinds of new awareness of meaning and thought.

Reading the Bible with a group helps us develop a discipline of study and can also give us increased confidence in approaching the Bible. The Bible is an intimidating book, and many people find it hard to trust their own interpretations. By reading the Bible with others, we come to trust our own ability to understand what the Scriptures are saying, and to learn the church's teachings about the Bible. In this dialogue between the church's teachings and our individual understandings of the Bible, new and deepening insight can take place.

Most Bible study methods, even those intended for individuals, can be adapted for use in groups. Each group needs to develop its own way of entering the Bible, and perhaps to explore several different methods over the course of their meetings.

Some Methods of Bible Study

Lectio Divina

The practice of prayerfully reading and reflecting on the Bible, both in common worship and in private study, was central to the daily life of the Benedictine monasteries of the Middle Ages. The purpose of this method known as *lectio divina* (holy or godly reading) was not primarily to increase one's knowledge of the Bible in the sense of an intellectual study; rather, monks practiced *lectio divina* as a devotional activity, as a means of being formed and shaped by the word of God.

In the words of the Benedictine scholar Norvene Vest, the foundation for *lectio divina* is "receptive attention." This sort of Scripture reading has the power not only to give new insights into the Bible, but to change our lives. *Lectio* is "the pattern of listening, response, and transformation. *Lectio* draws the reader ever more deeply into the encounter with Christ, which has concrete application in our life in a way that also transcends time."[1] Thus as we read the words of Scripture and reflect on them in the light of the troubles and joys we face on this day, in this moment, we allow God to speak new meanings, new insights. We see implications for our lives that we might never have seen before.

The actual practice of *lectio divina* varies from person to person, but in general it involves the reading of a passage of Scripture and a period of reflection on the words and meaning to be found there for one's life at this particular time. The writings of the Middle Ages often use the image of rumination to describe this process: just as a cow "ruminates" as she repeatedly chews her food, so we "ruminate"

---

1. Norvene Vest, *No Moment Too Small: Rhythms of Silence, Prayer, and Holy Reading* (Boston: Cowley Publications, 1994), 71, 78.

over the word of God in Scripture, taking a passage, a phrase, perhaps even one word and turning it over and over in our hearts and minds, all in the context of prayerful openness to God.

One common way of practicing *lectio divina* is to choose a passage from the Bible—which may be from the Daily Office Lectionary, if you are following those readings, or simply the next chapter in whatever book of the Bible you are reading through at this point in time. Begin reading, prayerfully and slowly, and when you come to a word or phrase that attracts your attention, stop. Repeat the word or phrase over and over, perhaps aloud so you can actually *hear* the words. Consider how this word or phrase might touch your life today. Why did it attract your attention? Did you find it troubling? A source of joy or comfort? Puzzling? How do you *feel* as you hear these words over and over again? Then consider what sort of invitation or opening God might be calling you to through this passage. How would you like to respond?

The practice of *lectio divina* can be incorporated into any structure of Bible reading you have undertaken, whether it be lectionary-based or simply reading a book straight through. It is a salutary reminder that our understanding of the Bible needs to be grounded both in a knowledge of the historical-critical methods of study that lead us to the literal meaning of the Scriptures and in an openness to the spiritual and allegorical meanings that form and inform our faith.

Three Senses of Scripture

Episcopal priest and scholar Michael Johnston has described an approach based in the long history of Christian interpretation of the Bible that he has found useful for studying the Bible both in groups and alone. He focuses on what he calls the "three senses of Scripture":

the literal, the historical, and the prophetic. No matter what particular method for Bible study is used, part of the study involves discernment of these three senses within the passage under consideration.

The *literal sense* of the passage is what the words of the text actually *say*, quite apart from any interpretation we might lay on them. It can be difficult to separate out the layers of assumptions and interpretations the church has placed on some passages of the Bible over the centuries, especially the more familiar or beloved ones. Johnston asks himself a few clarifying questions when looking for the literal sense: "What does this passage *really* say? Am I conflating the details, or mixing it up with some other passage? Am I bringing some particular point of view or bias to my reading?"

An obvious example of the significance of these layers of interpretation would be the well-known verse from Isaiah that speaks of the "sign" to be given to the house of David: "Look, the young woman is with child and shall bear a son, and shall name him Immanuel" (7:14). In the Greek Septuagint the Hebrew "young woman" is translated as "virgin," and it is this translation that the writer of Matthew's gospel used when he saw in Jesus's birth the fulfillment of this sign: "All this took place to fulfill what had been spoken by the Lord through the prophet: 'Look, the virgin shall conceive and bear a son, and they shall name him Emmanuel,' which means, 'God is with us'" (1:22–23). If we were seeking the literal sense of the passage from Isaiah, however, we would need to consider the Hebrew words themselves, not how they had been translated and interpreted at a later date or how we ourselves might wish to hear them.

The literal sense of the text leads quite naturally to the *historical sense*: What is the historical context in which the passage was written, and what did it mean to the people who heard it then? Knowing the historical context of the passage can inform our understanding of its meaning: some of the Psalms, for example, arose from royal court circles, and it is helpful to know something of the crises that shaped the reigns of the kings of Israel and Judah. Another, often inseparable, aspect of the historical sense is how the passage has been interpreted by people who heard it over the centuries, either as translators or worshipers or scholars. Jesus himself "reinterpreted" the Hebrew Scriptures in his teachings and life, such as when he refuses to stone the woman caught in adultery as would be required by Jewish law, and when he quotes Psalm 22 from the cross.

Likewise, knowing the history of the text itself can deepen our understanding of its historical sense—a study often known as textual criticism. Johnston cites an interesting example in one of Paul's letters, in which he forbids women to speak in church (1 Corinthians 14:33b–6). Since these verses are located in different places in the ancient manuscripts we have of that letter, and since they seem to contradict Paul's thoughts on the equality of women elsewhere in his letters, some scholars believe they were added at a later date, when the church was in the process of narrowing women's opportunities for leadership in the church community. When a word or a passage seems out of place or at odds with other writings, it is important to stop and investigate the history of the text. Sometimes these clues lead to significant changes in how we understand a particular book or writer.

The literal and historical senses both lay the foundation for the *prophetic sense* of Scripture. "To read the Bible for its prophetic sense," writes Michael Johnston, "is to use the text as an instrument for discerning God's presence in our lives now." When we ask questions like "What does this passage mean for us today?" "What is God saying to us in this passage?" "How should I respond to this passage?" we are seeking the prophetic, or spiritual, sense of the text. When the prophetic sense is separated from the literal or historical senses, we can find ourselves in realms of interpretation that are not grounded in the revelation of God in the Scriptures but are instead intensely and solely individualistic in meaning. On the other hand, as Johnston summarizes well, the prophetic or spiritual sense is essential for making meaning of the Bible:

> Reading for the literal alone tips toward fundamentalism, risking a future drawn upon an inadequate understanding of the past. But reading for the historical alone leaves us with little more than biblical archaeology; we end up knowing a good deal about ancient Israel but not very much about God. Reading for the spiritual alone tends toward the idiosyncratic and private; it looks to a future cut off from both the past and the present and can lead to strange and intensely personal interpretations. To appropriate the Bible fully, the believing community needs to read it for all three of its senses.[2]

African Bible Study

A popular way of approaching the Bible in churches today is known as the African Bible Study method. There are many variations of this method, which basically provides a way for groups to identify and focus on the three senses of Scriptures described above: the actual

---

2. Michael Johnston, *Engaging the Word*, vol. 3, New Church's Teaching Series (Cambridge, MA: Cowley Publications, 1998), 53.

words of the passage (the literal sense); its historical context and what it meant for the people to whom the words were written (the historical sense); and its meaning for us today (the prophetic sense). While this approach is designed primarily for studying the Bible in small groups, it can also be adapted for use by individuals or families at home.

Once a passage has been chosen—it might be from a daily lectionary or one of the readings assigned for the next Sunday, or simply one the group would like to study—the members of the group gather in a circle and three people volunteer to read the passage aloud. It is preferable to have a variety of voices, male and female, with a mixture of nationalities and ages, if possible.

After the first reader finishes reading the passage, each person in the group speaks aloud a word, phrase, or sentence that conveys an idea or image from the passage that particularly caught his or her attention. No commentary is allowed at this point, just simple impressions of what the words in the passage actually *say*—in other words, the group is gathering a sense of the literal meaning of the passage.

The second reader then reads the passage again. After this reading, anyone in the group may comment on its content or meaning. This is the time for more in-depth study, and the leader of the group may wish to bring commentaries, linguistic aids, and alternative translations into the discussion at this point. How did the original hearers of the passage interpret its meaning? Are there confusing or intriguing words we need to investigate? What can the historical context tell us? The group may wish to have on hand Bibles or written copies of the passage at this stage to enhance their study, since we are not as adept as our forebears in memorizing oral stories.

Finally, once the group has explored the historical and literal senses of the passage, the third reader again reads the passage aloud. Each member of the group then speaks aloud some sort of prayer or insight or desire for transformation gained through the hearing and studying of this passage. These prayers and reflections are then gathered by the group leader into a closing collect, reminding us that reading the Bible in the Christian community is always inextricably intertwined with prayer and transformation within the body of Christ.

Thematic Studies of Scripture

Another way to approach the Bible is to ask what it has to say about a particular topic, such as "righteousness" or "grace." This is a somewhat more challenging way to look at Scripture, and it can provide valuable insights for our understanding of the biblical story. To undertake this kind of study, a couple of reference materials are helpful. First, locate a concordance. A concordance lists words from the Bible alphabetically and gives all or the most important places those words appear in the Bible. The bigger the concordance, the more complete the list of words. Along with the words themselves, a concordance usually also provides a small portion of the verses in which the words appear. It may also indicate if there is more than one Hebrew or Greek root to the English translation.

If your theme is based upon a word, say "peace," you could look up the references to this word in a concordance and then compare the various ways it is used. In this case you might find that both Hebrew and Greek have a major word that is translated as "peace" in English Bibles, but that there are a couple of other terms that may also be translated "peace" in the sense of keeping silent (or "holding one's peace"). You would find only a few references to these minor words, but a long series of passages from many books of the Bible using the major words for "peace." By examining these texts a group or an individual could come to a much deeper understanding of what the Bible means when it speaks of the "peace of God."

Another helpful reference is a "wordbook" or Bible dictionary. Like a concordance, a Bible dictionary is arranged in alphabetical order, but rather than just listing all the passages in which the word appears, it will also offer a commentary on the meaning and biblical usage of the word or theme.

Such a thematic study of Scripture can be fruitful if the theme is one about which the Bible has something to say—of which there are many. But there are also themes that you would not find in the Bible in the direct sense of specific words used to speak about that theme. If you wanted to know what the Bible has to say about "creation," for example, you would find only a few references to that specific word in a concordance, while in a Bible dictionary you would find other more general references to the theme of creation in the Scriptures.

One word of caution. While these and other reference books can be helpful, they need to be used carefully. Often they will have their own particular descriptions of a theme or word. These insights can be helpful, but if you substitute reading *about* a theme for taking the time to locate the biblical references and reading them yourself, you risk coming only to the conclusions of a particular author and not to your own understanding. And, of course, the point of such a study is to come to know the Bible, not someone else's description of the Bible. The perceptions of other people, especially those who have a deep and scholarly knowledge of the Bible, will be helpful in filling in your own understanding, but the Bible must be the main text for study.

Literature Studies

Another way to come to a study of Scripture is to look at various kinds of biblical literature. As we have mentioned earlier, there are many kinds of literature in the Bible, and the ways in which biblical ideas and themes are presented is an important factor in understanding them. For example, a study of one of Paul's letters could well include some reflection on letter writing as a form of communication. The fact that Paul wrote in letters tells us something about his purpose and method. While his letters contain a great deal of what we think of as "doctrine," clearly Paul was not writing treatises or theological tomes. He chose to write letters, not gospels. His purpose was to address the situations in his churches, so his theological teachings come in the context of his reflection on what is actually happening, what is being said and taught in the congregations to whom he writes. Looking at Paul's teachings from this perspective can clarify some of his ideas and help create a context for his teachings that can be helpful in applying them to contemporary affairs.

Examining the kinds of literature in a biblical book or a section of a biblical book can be as important as looking at the words as you seek a perspective on the Bible's message. It can also help to illuminate the ways in which the people who wrote the Bible (and those to whom they wrote) thought about God and faith in their time. We can become more aware of how God communicates to his people through a variety of media. You may find that certain kinds of literature in the Bible speak more clearly to you than others. Perhaps poetry appeals to your way of thinking, or maybe you like stories or parables better. It may be that you prefer dialogue and discussion, or you may be the sort of person who likes difficult or abstract ideas. These are all present in the Scriptures, and finding them can help to draw you into the biblical story, thus leading you into a deeper connection with the Bible.

The Bible in the Arts

An interesting way to deepen an awareness of the Bible is to look at how the Bible has been used in literature and other art forms. Many poets and novelists throughout the history of western art have taken biblical themes as topics for their works. Among contemporary writers, John Steinbeck, William Faulkner, Frederick Buechner, Flannery O'Connor, John Updike, Annie Dillard, and others have written novels or short stories based upon biblical stories or ideas. Poets such as T. S. Eliot, W. H. Auden, and William Butler Yeats have likewise written poetry incorporating biblical themes and tales, and many artists, sculptors, and iconographers have portrayed biblical scenes or characters. These art forms can be ways for a group to begin to find connections with the biblical materials. In a sense, it is coming to Bible study from a different direction: instead of asking what the Bible says about our contemporary experience, we ask our experience and culture to lead us to and help us understand in a new way certain biblical truths or ideas. For example, there are several interesting studies of Rembrandt's famous painting of *The Prodigal Son*. By spending time looking at this painting—examining the people, discerning their attitudes, the expressions on their faces, and their connections with one another—the parable that Jesus tells in Luke 15:11–32 is brought to life in a new way. We can move from the simple words of the story to a deeper, more emotional engagement with the characters of the story. We see more clearly the God who is revealed in the parable, and we see ourselves more clearly, too.

Similarly, some of Flannery O'Connor's short stories can make interesting connections between the real world we live in and the world of the Bible. The poems of T. S. Eliot or the music of Bach or Mozart can also offer possibilities for experiencing various ways the biblical story has been expressed over time—expressions that go beyond the simple words of Scripture and speak not just to our minds, but to our hearts and our spirits as well.

In the past few years, a number of films have been produced that are directly connected to the biblical story, often arousing considerable controversy among people of faith. *The Passion of the Christ* is perhaps the most recent, but there are also films based on Jesus's parables, the book of Revelation, and the Exodus story. While there have been many attempts to create a visual telling of the stories of the Bible over the decades, with varying degrees of success, many films use such broader biblical themes as love, grace, redemption, and hope as a basis for telling a contemporary tale, one that evokes the Bible's voice without trying to reproduce it—perhaps sometimes even without realizing the universal themes conveyed are found in the Scriptures. These films often make for the best discussions and can be interesting ways to discover how Scripture actually speaks in the contemporary world.

Just Do It

So how do we approach, perhaps for the first time, a book that has engendered so many different methods of study and has fostered the development of an enormous library of supplementary resources and reference books? We just do it. We open the pages and start reading. Even if the words seem obscure or the stories strange, we keep reading. We ask questions. Talk with other people. Listen to sermons.

Find resources to help us. But above all, we keep reading. We are never reading alone in our reading of the Bible, for as Jesus told his disciples, God's Holy Spirit dwells within us to guide us into all truth (John 16:13). And so we trust that no matter how sketchy or inadequate our knowledge of the Bible is now, we will still be able to hear God's word in these sometimes obscure or strange words. What matters is simply that we open this big, intimidating, wonderful book—and listen with our ears attuned and our eyes open to see the God revealed there.

3 ▪ Learning from the Liturgical Year

We seem to have a problem with time. We want it to pass more slowly or more quickly, seldom satisfied with its appointed pace. Children, for whom experienced time passes slowly, would usually like to speed things up: They can scarcely wait for Christmas or their birthday or summer vacation to arrive. Adults, too, can find the passage of time tedious: prisoners, family members awaiting the return of a loved one, passengers stuck in an airport, those afflicted with burdensome illness, and residents of convalescent homes. We devise ways to "pass the time" or, worse, "kill time." At least by middle age, however, most adults would like time to slow down. After all, we know where it is heading. And if we fear a future that inevitably spells death, backward reflection is often no better, either because the past holds painful memories or because the irretrievable loss of beloved people, places, and occasions triggers aching nostalgia.

Toward the end of *Macbeth*, Shakespeare's protagonist anguishes over the ruthless course of time:

> To-morrow, and to-morrow, and to-morrow,
>
> Creeps in this petty pace from day to day
>
> To the last syllable of recorded time;
>
> And all our yesterdays have lighted fools
>
> The way to dusty death.
>
> Out, out, brief candle!
>
> Life's but a walking shadow, a poor player
>
> That struts and frets his hour upon the stage

And then is heard no more.

It is a tale Told by an idiot, full of sound and fury,

Signifying nothing. (Act V, Scene V, 19–28)

Even if we do not share Macbeth's final nihilism, his speech poignantly expresses our useless protest against time's gradual but inexorable march: "To-morrow, and to-morrow, and to-morrow/ Creeps in this petty pace from day to day." Little by little time eats away at our lives, and we can do nothing to stop it. We enjoy, perhaps, our "hour upon the stage" of life, but then we must make our exit, leaving room for other actors to take our place until they, too, must depart.

In itself, of course, time is neither threatening nor benign, although just what time is has puzzled many a philosopher or scientist. It is only as it affects conscious creatures, who move from birth to growth to maturation to decay and finally death, that time seems like an enemy. And as creatures uniquely endowed with the capacity to reflect on time, we are left wondering why we yearn for longevity—if not immortality—when it is beyond our grasp. Several voices within Scripture lament the brevity of life, but perhaps none more eloquently than Psalm 90:

> You turn us back to the dust and say, "Go back,
>   O child of earth."
>
> For a thousand years in your sight are like yesterday
>   when it is past
>
> and like a watch in the night. You sweep us away
>   like a dream;
>
> we fade away suddenly like the grass.

In the morning it is green and flourishes;

In the evening it is dried up and withered . . .

The span of our life is seventy years,

perhaps in strength even eighty;

yet the sum of them is but labor and sorrow,

for they pass away quickly and we are gone. (3–6, 10)

Yet meditation upon the transience of life does not drive the psalmist to despair, as it does for Macbeth, but to faith. Given the brief span of life, the psalmist prays for wisdom to use the remaining days well: "So teach us to number our days /that we may apply our hearts to wisdom" (v.12) and "prosper the work of our hands; /prosper our handiwork" (v.17). Trust in God enlivens the daily round, even though it must come to an end: "so shall we rejoice and be glad all the days of our life" (v.14). We can accept the life we have as gift, rendering thanks for it with joy. Only for God are "a thousand years . . . like yesterday."

God resolves our problem with time by entering it: "when the fullness of time had come, God sent his Son, born of a woman, born under the law, in order to redeem those who were under the law, so that we might receive adoption as children" (Galatians 4:4–5). If the limitations of time frustrate our longings, writing an absolute "the end" upon the final chapter of our life, God breaks into these very constrictions through the Word made flesh. Jesus enters into the finitude of our lot.

The Christian liturgical year marks by its annual cycle key phases in this "fullness of time." It traces Jesus's earthly movement through time and beyond time, starting with the coming of Christ into the world and ending with his ascension and gift of the Spirit. In its early stages, the church calendar began with observance of the great festivals of the Christian Pascha (Easter and Pentecost) as well as Epiphany. It then grew to encompass the whole spectrum of events from Jesus's birth to his glorification. As we pass through the days of our life, then, both individually and collectively, we become ever more immersed in Christ's life. Our brief time on earth is thus sanctified and charged with eternity.

While baptism initiates us into Christ's own life, a crucial means by which we continue growing into that life is through the annual observance of its pivotal moments, especially those marking Jesus's birth, baptism, death, rising, and glorification. These events, while belonging on one plane to the realm of history, are considered "mysteries"—not because they are an inscrutable enigma, but because they have eternal significance and infinite depth. In the New Testament, the word *"mystērion"* signifies something that human beings could not know except by divine revelation: Once hidden, it is now revealed in Christ, though we can never fully probe its inexhaustible meaning. Precisely because the whole mystery of Christ is so vast and multifaceted, the major feasts and seasonal celebration of the particular events of Christ's life are spread across the year.

It is through the liturgies of the Daily Office and the Holy Eucharist, above all, that we experience the distinct flavor of each liturgical season. The lessons appointed for both office and Eucharist change markedly in tone from one season to the next, inviting us to ponder the particular mystery of Christ commemorated in that season. Seasonal or festal antiphons in the office, hymns suitable to the day or season, and alterations in the color of vestments and decor all contribute to the usually subtle but sometimes dramatic shift from one liturgical season to the next. Like the change of seasons in the natural world, these variations are psychologically satisfying. In the northern hemisphere, where the liturgical year developed, the variations in sunlight over the course of the year reinforce the drama of the church's unfolding liturgical seasons. As in the natural world much remains the same: the structure of the liturgy is little altered. But the small differences add up, lending a distinctive coloration to each church season. The liturgical year allows us to move interiorly not so much in a cycle as in a spiral, every year plunging deeper into the mystery of Christ.

Woven into this annual round are the commemorations of particular saints. These are our spiritual friends who, across the threshold of time and death, offer us encouragement by their example: They lived into the mystery of Christ, each in his or her unique way, to an extraordinary degree. Some—the martyrs—witnessed to Christ in the face of death. Others lay down their lives in loving service, from care for the poor to missionary zeal to theological scholarship. Saints are found in every generation and in every walk of life. Some saints have left their writings to teach and inspire us; others are known through the legends and stories that grew up around them. Although the saints in our calendar lived in the past, they really belong to the future, for they illustrate the horizons of holiness and wisdom to which we are called in Christ.

Advent

As in ordinary English usage, Advent refers to a "coming." But which one? It turns out that the brief season of Advent is exceptionally thick with meaning. While most people, both in the church and outside it, think of Advent as a time of preparation for Christmas—the first "coming" of Christ into the world—the liturgies for Advent focus more on our Lord's final coming at the end of time. This eschatological orientation in the appointed collects and readings gets underway about a month before Advent even begins, officially at least, which is usually on the last Sunday of November. Advent, then, has a long run up to it.

The month of November comes late in autumn. In the temperate zones, early fall days are typically colorful and crisp, but by late autumn trees are largely stripped of leaves and dampness sets in. The days become shorter, darker, and colder. Ancient peoples responded to these natural occurrences, resulting as we know now from the earth's rotation around the sun, by enacting rituals to coax the sun god's return or to appease the spirits of the dead. Contemporary customs around Halloween seem to enact a modern-day version of the attempt to scare death to death. Reveling in the macabre and gruesome, in witches, ghosts, and things that go bump in the night, bespeaks a need to face the universal fear of death. It is no accident that this occurs as the cycle of nature, and even the sunlight, seems to fail, undergoing a kind of death. Late autumn is *memento mori* writ large.

Halloween, of course, is "All Hallows Eve," the night before All Saints' Day, November 1. The saints who have completed their course bear testimony to Christ's final victory: deliverance from death and the defeat of evil. The grace of Jesus's resurrection shines through them. Originally a feast of all the martyrs—the witnesses to Christ par excellence—All Saints' Day later came to celebrate other Christians of exemplary virtue. Since everyone needs models to inspire and emulate, All Saints' Day holds before us this "great cloud of witnesses." Its celebration might prompt us to delve still deeper: to become acquainted with the saints by reading some of their works or the writings about them, drawing wisdom and encouragement for our spiritual journey.

November 2 serves as something of an extension of the Feast of All Saints as the church commemorates All Faithful Departed—All Souls' Day, as it is popularly known. Unlike All Saints, this day has a domestic feel about it, as we hold in prayer, often with a twinge of sadness, our beloved dead: family members and friends passed from this world to the next. The Mexican "Day of the Dead," itself built upon Aztec foundations, embraces all three days in a unified remembrance of friends and ancestors.

With this eschatological horizon now before us, the readings for the last weeks of Pentecost sharpen the vision of the end of time by turning to "last things." The Scripture lessons for both Eucharist and Office have a somber tone. Predictions of the destruction of the temple, and parables about the return of Christ and the last judgment, dominate this season. While many in the church today shrink from contemplating the theme of judgment, assuming that it only spells condemnation, the insistence in both the Old and New Testaments on a final reckoning is actually an assurance that divine justice and truth will prevail in the end. In a world riddled by lies and cruelties, where the cries of the powerless often go unheard, the conviction that Christ will come again is grounds for hope. The lessons for the Last Sunday after Pentecost bring the season to a close with the climactic image of Christ the King, treated from various angles over the three-year Sunday lectionary.

The First Sunday of Advent seamlessly continues these themes, now adding the further dimension of apocalyptic. Here the birth pangs of the new creation are described in terms of cosmic catastrophe, with the sun becoming dark and stars falling from heaven. This dramatic imagery augurs the coming reign of God. The watchword here, and indeed throughout Advent, is vigilance: "Keep awake!" The stern figure of John the Baptist appears in gospels for the Second and Third Sundays of Advent, calling us, as he did his contemporaries, to repentance. His preaching prepared Israel for the advent of Jesus; his summons to renewal prepares us for the second advent of Christ as well as for the celebration of Christmas. It is only with the Fourth Sunday of Advent that the church turns our attention to that festival with pre-Nativity gospels, focused on the figures of Mary and Joseph.

As is the case with every liturgical season, Advent underscores aspects of our life in Christ that are true throughout the year. Yet each season brings them into sharper focus. Vigilance, for instance, is a crucial spiritual practice. It demands that we pay attention to what is going on inside us and around us, discerning what is of God and what is not. Naturally this leads—as John the Baptist would tell us—to ongoing repentance. Vigilance also embraces the holy expectation of meeting Christ, sometimes when we least anticipate it. The Collect for the Fourth Sunday of Advent speaks of God's "daily visitation":

> Purify our conscience, Almighty God, by your daily visitation, that your Son Jesus Christ, at his coming, may find in us a mansion prepared for himself . . . (BCP, 212)

Here, as in many of the Advent prayers, the "comings" of Christ are intertwined: the first coming in his incarnation, his final coming at the end of history, and his coming at the intersection with the everyday. This last sense, issuing in constant vigilance for the appearing of Christ, has sometimes been called the "sacrament of the present moment."

The spirituality of Advent is marked by urgent longing: "O that you would tear open the heavens and come down" (Isaiah 64:1) begins one of its lessons. Advent allows us to acknowledge the incompleteness of things, since the world as we know it is plainly far from perfect. Those who "hunger and thirst for righteousness" embody Advent spirituality as they yearn for the coming of Christ to establish his kingdom forever. In much the same way, Advent gives scope to our dreams. The extraordinary picture of the "Peaceable Kingdom" in Isaiah 11:1–10 combines hope of a messianic ruler with perfect harmony in the animal world, where "the wolf shall live with the lamb, the leopard shall lie down with the kid, the calf and the lion and the fatling together." The American Quaker and folk artist Edward Hicks (1780–1849) was so taken with this vision—quite impossible in the present order of nature—that he painted over sixty versions of it.

Closer to our time, Martin Luther King Jr. also famously had a "dream" of justice in his land. When our dreams coincide with God's, when we are dissatisfied with present violence, when we can imagine the shape of justice, we live in an Advent spirit, no matter the time of year. The invocation, "Our Lord, come!" was ever the prayer of the early church.

Christmas

"At midnight there was a cry, 'Behold, the bridegroom! Come out to meet him'" (Matthew 25:6). At Christmas there is a turn, in nature and in the church. Since the New Testament does not indicate when Jesus was born, in the fourth century the church settled the Feast of the Nativity of our Lord to coincide with the winter solstice. No doubt a pastoral strategy lay behind this liturgical date, intended to counter prevailing pagan festivities. But there was a more compelling reason, too: The occasion of the solstice illustrated how "the true light, which enlightens everyone, was coming into the world" (John 1:9). Christmas Midnight Mass is celebrated in the darkest hours of the night. Yet the light of Christ pierces and illumines the darkness of the world, and turns it around. The Prologue of St. John's Gospel, always read on the First Sunday after Christmas, supplies this cosmic background to the Christmas story, as does the hymn "Of the Father's Love Begotten," whose opening stanza echoes this gospel:

> Of the Father's love begotten, ere the worlds began
>   to be,
>
> he is Alpha and Omega, he the source, the ending he,
>
> of the things that are, that have been,
>
> and that future years shall see, evermore and
>   evermore!

The tender domesticity of the Nativity story brings home the nearness of God as Emmanuel, "God-with-us." Because people often fear that God is distant, perhaps uncaring, the gift of the Incarnation is something to be savored, pondered long in meditation. God comes to us in the flesh, as vulnerable and unthreatening as a baby. Moreover, the naked helplessness of the newborn child, the hardships of Mary and Joseph, and the menacing cruelty of Herod, all link the Nativity narratives to the Passion narratives. Christmas points ahead to its culmination in the Paschal mystery. Christ was born to save us.

Precisely because many of the traditional Christmas hymns are familiar to us from years of repetition, we can easily overlook the theological strength that informs several of them. Consider, for example, the third stanza of Charles Wesley's "Hark! the herald angels sing":

> Mild he lays his glory by, born that we no more
>   may die,
> born to raise us from the earth, born to give us
>   second birth.

These well-known lines skillfully juxtapose birth and death: Christ's birth to extinguish death. Following the Philippians' hymn (2:5–11), Wesley invites meditation on Christ's self-abasement for the sake of our salvation. He also plays with birth imagery as he writes of Jesus's human birth for our spiritual rebirth: "born to give us second birth." In much the same vein, the lessons during Christmastide press us to realize Christ's birth within ourselves: "But when the fullness of time had come, God sent his Son, born of a woman, born under the law, in order to redeem those who were under the law, so that we might receive adoption as children" (Galatians 4:4–5). Entering into the Christmas mystery, then, includes the ardent desire that Christ be born in us, his life constantly shaping our own. Phillips Brooks captures this prayer in the final stanza of "O little town of Bethlehem": "O holy Child of Bethlehem, descend to us, we pray; cast out our sin and enter in, *be born in us today*."

In a culture such as ours that understands Christmas very little and Advent not at all, the observance of these discrete seasons can be awkward for Christians to negotiate. But there is much to be lost in blurring their distinction in an amorphous "holiday season" that kicks off at Thanksgiving, if not at Halloween. We need to hear the Advent stress upon vigilance, a vigilance nurtured by quiet and silence. When a great deal of contemporary religion is artificially sunny, Advent's sober acceptance of darkness, waiting, incompleteness, and contemplative longing offers a unique perspective and grace. It grounds us in reality.

When Advent is observed in its integrity, the Twelve Days of Christmas can be celebrated as the festive season it is. This is the time for Christmas decoration and parties at home and at church. There are also major feast days scattered in the Christmastide season. We can let the joy of the Incarnation seep in. Theologians and poets have reveled in the paradoxes of Christmas: the Creator becoming a creature, the Infinite inhabiting the finite—in Mary's body, in the church, and in the world. The paradox of Christmas can take hold of us, too, as we continually invite Christ to be born in us, to grow in us and, as we turn to Epiphany, to be manifest in us.

Epiphany

The Feast of the Epiphany, observed on January 6, is one of the most ancient solemnities in the church. Originally, it celebrated the baptism of our Lord, and in the Eastern Orthodox Church, it still does. In the Western church, Epiphany marks the visit of the magi to the infant Jesus (Matthew 2:1–12). Both these events are rightly considered "epiphanies" or "manifestations" of Christ (Greek *epiphania*, manifestation). With his baptism Jesus emerged from obscurity to begin his public ministry. At that very moment, he is manifested as the Son of God and the Messiah. The Orthodox also refer to the baptism as a "theophany" of the triune God. Here the Trinity is explicitly revealed as the Spirit descends upon Jesus, anointing him as the Christ, while the Father's voice claims him as his beloved.

In its calendar, the Episcopal Church joins with Western observance in commemorating the visit of the magi on January 6. As "wise men from the East," the magi represent the Gentile world. Christ's manifestation to these seekers of truth prefigures the later apostolic mission to the non-Jewish world; embedded in the birth narrative is this hint of the universality of the gospel. Still, the Feast of the Baptism of our Lord is not by any means overlooked: our church calendar significantly places it on the First Sunday after the Epiphany, thus yoking Eastern and Western church traditions. As we have already seen in chapter 1, the baptism of our Lord is of immense import for all who have been baptized into Christ. It is therefore one of the four feast days recommended for Holy Baptism (BCP, 312).

Having passed the winter solstice, the days gradually grow longer in the months of January and February. The Epiphany season builds on the impression of "light coming into the world" as the Sunday gospels proclaim the calling of the apostles, the early teaching and healing ministry of Jesus, or the Sermon on the Mount. The manifestation of Jesus presses forward; the kingdom of God is breaking in. That light now must penetrate and illumine our minds, hearts, and actions. A seasonal blessing sums up the grace of Epiphany: "May Christ, the Son of God, be manifest in you, that your lives may be a light to the world" (*The Book of Occasional Services*, 24).

The Epiphany season ends with the climactic epiphany of the Transfiguration. While the Feast of the Transfiguration of our Lord occurs in the summer (August 6), the gospels for the Last Sunday after the Epiphany bring forward this radiant moment of glory just as we are about to embark upon Lent. The Baptism of our Lord and his Transfiguration thus frame the Epiphany season. In the gospel accounts, the heavenly voice owns Jesus as "My Son, the Beloved" or "My Son, my Chosen." Here on the holy mountain Jesus, shining with unearthly light, is revealed in his divine glory. This dazzling epiphany comes toward the conclusion of Jesus's Galilean ministry. He is about to "set his face" toward Jerusalem, where he will suffer and die. The story of the Transfiguration signals a crucial turning point in the gospel narratives, and its placement at the end of the Epiphany season signals a decisive turning point for the church, too. With his chosen disciples, we are graced to apprehend Jesus transfigured with divine light before we see him disfigured in the darkness of his passion. At this juncture, we briefly glimpse the resurrection glory awaiting Jesus—and us—at the end of Lent.

Lent

"Remember that you are dust, and to dust you shall return." Lent begins with the somber recognition of our mortality. We celebrate the Resurrection at Easter only after facing squarely the inevitability of death. What we make of death determines what we make of life. In our death-denying culture, in which youth is extolled and getting old is considered a misfortune, Ash Wednesday is strangely liberating. The ashes are smeared upon our foreheads in the sign of the cross—the same sign with which chrism anoints our foreheads at baptism. All of Lent is moving towards the passion and resurrection of Jesus, culminating at Easter with baptisms or the renewal of baptism. Lent prepares us for this grace by taking us into the mystery of the cross, our bridge from death to life. It is the season to probe sources of bondage and diminishment: What feels like death just now? What is holding us back from fullness of life in Christ? Our renewing of baptism entails searching self-examination and repentance. We must undergo a death to sin and all forms of resistance to God.

The forty days of Lent have several biblical antecedents: Jesus's forty-day fast after his baptism; the Israelites' forty-year sojourn in the wilderness; even the forty days and nights of torrential rain in the Great Flood. These stories are connected: temptation, sin, and renewal are threads running through them in various configurations. Jesus's victory over the Tempter prefigures his final victory over evil on the cross. That Jesus was "tempted in every way as we are, yet did not sin" (BCP, 379; Hebrews 4:15) is a consoling and heartening Lenten motif. Our weakness is buttressed by his strength.

The traditional disciplines of Lent—prayer, fasting, and almsgiving—are salutary habits inherited from Jewish piety, although the last two practices require some interpretation. Prayer, of course, is a fundamental discipline for Christians. Without it, we do not know God or live in Christ. Baptism commits us to corporate and private prayer: "the breaking of bread and the prayers." So if we have been negligent in eucharistic worship, in the prayer of the church (traditionally the Daily Office), or in setting aside time for personal prayer, resuming or enhancing these practices will be the obvious place for our Lenten discipline to begin.

The Episcopal Church designates only two days as "fasts": Ash Wednesday and Good Friday. In the Bible and in early centuries of the church, fasting meant refraining from food and drink until sundown, when a simple meatless meal would be taken. Over time, the Western church has greatly mitigated the discipline of fasting to entail two small meals and one meatless meal. By contrast, Muslims today engage in a complete fast, abstaining even from water, every day of Ramadan. Since there are now different traditions of fasting in the church, just how we practice it will depend upon our work and state of health, as we weigh the spiritual benefits of a more or less rigorous fast.

Abstinence refers to omitting certain foods or pleasures for the purpose of self-denial. Since all the weekdays of Lent and Holy Week and all Fridays throughout the year, except in the seasons of Christmas and Easter, are deemed "Days of Special Devotion" (BCP, 17), many Christians practice some form of abstinence on these days. Traditional forms of abstinence involve refraining from meat or alcohol. The Eastern Orthodox continue to require eliminating meat and all animal products throughout the Great Lent.

But what is the purpose of denying ourselves legitimate pleasures? At one level it trains the will. By occasionally denying ourselves innocent gratifications, we become more spiritually fit to deny ourselves the illicit ones. But on another level bodily self-denial constitutes a form of praying with the body. It expresses penitence and desire for conversion of life. We feel our weakness in cravings for pleasures to which we have become accustomed. We may grow more compassionate towards those who must "do without" every day of their lives. We sense in our very bodies utter dependence upon God, the giver of all gifts, and we realize anew our overwhelming need for grace to uphold us in our frailty.

Since alienation from our bodies is, oddly enough, an upshot of the sedentary and soft lifestyle of the affluent, it is worth asking ourselves as Lent approaches: What "fullness of life" might God wish for me? Contrary to the popular stereotype, St. Paul teaches that the body bears immense dignity because of our union with Christ in the resurrection—something that conditions our bodies even now. He further reminds us: "Do you not know that your body is a temple of the Holy Spirit within you, which you have from God, and that you are not your own? For you were bought with a price; therefore glorify God in your body" (1 Corinthians 6:19–20). If we are to "glorify

God in the body," what would that look like? Clearly, it would call us to relinquish habits that damage the body such as smoking, excessive or unhealthful eating and drinking, and failure to exercise. St. Paul is not here advocating the cultus of beautiful bodies so prevalent in today's advertising. He is rather pleading for honoring the body, offering a persuasive theological rationale for treating it with respect: the resurrection of the body governs how we regard the body. Nowadays, too, we need to consider the body of the earth so as to take into account the environmental impact of our food choices. Lent, then, can initiate a recovery of balance that leads to Easter joy. It could begin the hard process of undoing injurious habits that would continue the rest of the year.

"Almsgiving" sounds quaint to our ears, but in traditional religious culture it is a pillar of practical piety. While at first glance it might seem to smack of *noblesse oblige*, the obligation laid upon the rich to give alms binds them tangibly to the poor. Sharing wealth enacts how we belong to each other in community. While acknowledging the unequal distribution of material goods among people, the Scriptures seek to lessen the burden on the poor by various provisions. Or as the prophet Micah summarizes the core of Old Testament teaching: "What does the Lord require of you but to do justice, and to love kindness, and to walk humbly with your God?" (6:8). Jesus further developed this tradition by frequently teaching about wealth, warning about its danger to ensnare: "For where your treasure is, there your heart will be also" (Matthew 6:21). In other words, if you want an accurate gauge of your values, "follow the money." Just how Christians should practice economic justice persists as a vexing issue. But our duty to seek some measure of fairness in this crucial aspect of our common life remains. The social fabric of community demands it.

When writing to the Corinthians about a collection he is organizing for the poor in Jerusalem, Paul sets sensible limits to giving: Members of the church, he assures them, are under no obligation to impoverish themselves in order to assist others. Rather, he says, "it is a question of a fair balance between your present abundance and their need" (2 Corinthians 8:13–14). What that "fair balance" might mean in our own circumstances is a hard question with which we must wrestle. But cultivating the habit of generosity—"almsgiving"—is a way to begin.

Holy Week

By the end of Lent our eyes are fixed on Jesus. Everything in Lent, our personal observances and the liturgies of the church, has been preparing us for its culmination in Holy Week. Through the solemn liturgies of Holy Week, we participate in those events by which we and the entire world are saved. At times, these services can seem emotionally and physically exhausting, and rightly so. We will not easily be remade in Christ. The week begins with the gripping drama of The Sunday of the Passion: Palm Sunday. Here we feel our vacillation as we shift from "Hosanna" to "Crucify him!" Yet the faithfulness of Jesus, who "loved us to the end," reveals itself at every point in the passion narrative. Each day of this week is termed "holy," but none more so than the final three days: the Triduum. The observances on Maundy Thursday, Good Friday, and the Great Vigil of Easter really amount to one continuous liturgy. Unless some urgent obligation prevents us from attending, we should be present at this momentous liturgy in all three parts. For here, more than anywhere else, we "pass over" with Christ from death to life. We become again people of the Resurrection.

Easter

The Easter gospels begin with the astonished women at the tomb. We remain thunderstruck at the Easter proclamation: "Alleluia. Christ is risen." We hear it, but find it hard to take in. Like the apostles listening to the women's report, deep down we may suspect this gospel to be too good to be true.

The risen Lord is a mysterious figure. As we observed earlier, even those closest to him fail, at first, to realize who he is. There seems to be both continuity and discontinuity with the Jesus of Nazareth they once knew. Now risen, Jesus comes and goes as he pleases. He can be in more than one place at the same time. He accompanies two disciples en route to Emmaus, yet on the same day appears to Simon Peter back in Jerusalem (Luke 24:33–35). Locked doors are no obstacle to him: he passes right through them (John 20:19). In the garden where she first encounters the risen Lord, Mary Magdalene wants, literally, to hold on to Jesus, but cannot (John 20:17). Yet in his risen state Jesus still maintains an intimacy with his disciples. He speaks with them and, most significantly, eats with them.

The resurrection narratives offer tantalizing glimpses of what the resurrection might mean, both for Jesus and for us. The resurrection of Jesus is altogether different from the raising of Lazarus (John 11:1–44), which serves in the Gospel of John as a "sign" pointing to the resurrection of Jesus. But that miracle, though astounding, is still not an instance of resurrection itself. Lazarus, after all, was raised to ordinary mortal life, and he would eventually die again. In the resurrection, Jesus is no resuscitated corpse. The resurrection does not simply put him back together again like Humpty Dumpty in the nursery rhyme. His humanity has changed. In the risen Christ, we witness the beginning of the new creation. Jesus is no longer bound by death or, for that matter, the limitations of space and time. He is recognizably human and bodily, but his humanity is transfigured.

Other Christians before us have wondered just what the resurrection might mean. Evidently even in the first century, Christians in Corinth struggled with this issue. Fortunately for us, Paul devotes considerable thought to drawing out the implications of the resurrection in his first letter to them. Like many of us, the Corinthians were asking, "How are the dead raised? With what kind of body do they come?" (1 Corinthians 15:35). In his reply, Paul employs an agricultural metaphor, comparing a corpse to a seed that is sown, which must first disintegrate: "What you sow does not come to life unless it dies. And as for what you sow, you do not sow the body that is to be, but a bare seed, perhaps of wheat or of some other grain" (1 Cor. 15:36–37). What springs to life at harvest time is so vastly different from the simple seed that was planted that it appears to us as something altogether different:

> So it is with the resurrection of the dead. What is sown is perishable, what is raised is imperishable. It is sown in dishonor, it is raised in glory. It is sown in weakness, it is raised in power. It is sown a physical body, it is raised a spiritual body. If there is a physical body, there is also a spiritual body. (1 Corinthians 15:42–44)

Jesus uses much the same metaphor to speak of his impending death in St. John's gospel—a gospel written decades after Paul's first letter to the Corinthians: "The hour has come for the Son of Man to be glorified. Very truly, I tell you, unless a grain of wheat falls into the earth and dies, it remains just a single grain; but if it dies, it bears much fruit" (John 12:23–24). The similarity to Paul may just be coincidental, or perhaps Paul is drawing on an oral tradition going back to Jesus himself.

In any case, the metaphor of the dying seed in both instances suggests both continuity and radical change. There is continuity: the risen Jesus is, finally, recognizable as the man Jesus of Nazareth. They are not two different people. Yet Jesus is profoundly altered. He is no longer constrained by the ordinary limitations of this world. He has what Paul calls a "spiritual body" (*sōma pneumatikon*). By this unusual term, Paul does not intend to evoke some sort of insubstantial, diaphanous body—the kind of "body" with which ghosts are usually portrayed. He means that the resurrection body is a real body shot through and through with the Spirit. Now liberated from mortality, it is no longer bound by any earthly restriction.

Because Jesus is risen and ascended, many things become possible. We can encounter him anywhere and anytime. He is present in the members of his body, the church, of which he is the head (Ephesians 4:15). He dwells in the least of his brothers and sisters. He meets us in the sacraments and in prayer. Indeed, he "fills all things" (Ephesians 4:10). The resurrection of Jesus affects everything and everyone. The whole universe is changed by the one who defeated death, a creation that has always been "groaning in travail" because it is subject to the "futility" of eventual decay and death:

> For the creation waits with eager longing for the revealing of the children of God; for the creation was subjected to futility, not of its own will but by the will of the one who subjected it, in hope that the creation itself will be set free from its bondage to decay and will obtain the freedom of the glory of the children of God. We know that the whole

creation has been groaning in labor pains until now; and not only the creation, but we ourselves, who have the first fruits of the Spirit, groan inwardly while we wait for adoption, the redemption of our bodies. (Romans 8:19–23)

Paul's cosmic vision here anticipates what contemporary thinkers call the "web of nature." As John Muir famously said, "When we try to pick out anything by itself, we find it hitched to everything else in the universe." Since humans are part of creation, we stand in solidarity with the rest of nature, whether plants, animals, stars, or galaxies. Together we suffer from "bondage to decay," awaiting the full redemption of our bodies. So we are connected to creation, but we are also connected to Christ. What we have now received of resurrection grace is the "first fruits of the Spirit," and that is enough to anchor our hope. Hope is not wishful thinking, but rather a dimension of faith that is continually nurtured by contact with the risen Lord.

Throughout Easter Week and the Great Fifty Days of this season, the lessons help us identify *how* the risen Lord is present with us so that we, too, can recognize him and believe. The first gift of the risen Lord is forgiveness. Since Jesus's resurrection overcomes evil, even the most dire situations can be made new. The possibility of forgiveness is released into the world. So when Jesus appears to his fearful and guilty disciples—their locked doors are no barrier to him—he bears a message of peace and forgiveness: "Peace be with you" and "Receive the Holy Spirit. If you forgive the sins of any, they are forgiven them" (John 20:21–23; Gospel for Easter 2). Jesus then eats with his disciples when they gather, or by the seashore, or at Emmaus. We know him in the breaking of bread. For many, regular encounter with Christ in the Eucharist is the very ground of their faith in him. On the Fourth Sunday of Easter, we listen over the three years to different portions of John 10. Jesus is our Good Shepherd, who knows each of us by name. We recognize his voice, and follow where he leads.

Gospels for the last Sundays of the Easter season are taken from the "Farewell Discourses" of St. John's gospel. These speak of ongoing communion between Jesus and his disciples: "I am the vine, you are the branches." Several speak of the promised Spirit: "The Advocate, the Holy Spirit . . . will teach you everything, and remind you of all that I have said to you." All these gospels, and the other Easter lessons in the Daily Office and in the eucharistic lectionary, offer ample material for our meditation. The risen Lord lives in us, "abides" in us, and in the church.

Forty days after Easter, following Lukan chronology, the church celebrates the Feast of the Ascension. For many people the Ascension is problematic, if they think about it at all. Some dismiss the premodern cosmology by which the event is described (Acts 1:9); others wonder what there is to celebrate. Yet the Ascension of our Lord is a crucial aspect of the Easter mystery. It portrays Jesus's glorification in his return to the Father. The New Testament indicates that the resurrection appearances eventually ceased, but Jesus did not go away. "And remember, I am with you always, to the end of the age" are our Lord's final words in St. Matthew's gospel (28:20). Indeed, the whole Easter season has been revealing just how we encounter him now.

In the Ascension, Jesus's glorification is completed; and in that glorification, we have a share. As in the vision on the Mount of Transfiguration, we apprehend in Jesus our own eschatological destiny. For the Epistle to the Ephesians, this future glory catches us up even now: "But God, who is rich in mercy, out of the great love with which he loved us even when we were dead in our trespasses, made us alive together with Christ—by grace you have been saved—*and raised us up with him and seated us with him in the heavenly places in Christ Jesus*" (2:4–6). The Ascension of our Lord therefore celebrates our glory in Christ: where Jesus is, there we are. In his hymn for this feast day, "See the Conqueror mounts in triumph," Christopher Wordsworth notes this twofold glorification in the final stanza:

> Thou hast raised our human nature on the clouds to
>   God's right hand:
>
> there we sit in heavenly places, there with thee in
>   glory stand.
>
> Jesus reigns, adored by angels, Man with God is on
>   the throne;
>
> mighty Lord, in thine ascension, we by faith behold
>   our own.

Pentecost brings the Easter season to a climactic close. With Mary and the disciples we receive anew the gift of the Holy Spirit. In the Acts of the Apostles, as we observed in chapter 1, the immediate effect of the Spirit upon the gathered community is a vigorous proclamation of Christ's resurrection. The apostolic mission begins with a newfound fearlessness in the face of persecution and death. For the resurrection of Jesus dispels our ultimate fear: fear of death. The Spirit brings the resurrection home, transforming disciples into apostles. Following a somewhat different tradition, St. John's gospel also explicitly links Jesus's glorification with the outpouring of the Spirit (John 7:39). After the resurrection and as a consequence of it, the mission of God in sending Jesus is perpetuated in Jesus's commissioning of disciples: "As the Father has sent me, so I send you. . . . Receive the Holy Spirit." The risen Lord then breathes on them, effecting a new creation (John 20:21–22; cf. Genesis 2:7).

Yet before any of this happens, the Risen Lord first shows his disciples "his hands and his side." A week later he invites Thomas to place his finger in his wounded hands and his hand into his pierced side. Even in resurrection glory, the wounds remain. History inflicts scars. The tradition of placing five incense grains in the paschal candle, representing the five wounds of Jesus, witnesses to this insight. The grace of the resurrection, then, imparts no instant cheery optimism. Such an expectation can be burdensome. People sometimes doubt the sincerity of their faith if, as believers in the resurrection, they still experience anxiety, fear, or discouragement. The resurrection is our final horizon; it places suffering in perspective. But suffering persists. As Julian of Norwich testifies of Christ near the end of her revelations: "He said not, 'Thou shalt not be tempted; thou shalt not be troubled; thou shalt not be distressed,' but He said, 'Thou shalt not be overcome.'" The resurrection instills strength and courage. It grounds us in hope to persevere, as Jesus did, to the end.

Time after Pentecost

With the Christmas cycle and the Easter cycle now completed, the first Sunday after Pentecost is Trinity Sunday. Our contemplation moves towards the triune God: the One from whom and towards whom the events of salvation, just now celebrated, have their origin and goal. When everything is finally subjected to God, "God may be all in all" (1 Corinthians 15:28).

For roughly the next six months, we will be in the "green" season of church décor and slow, organic growth. Our readings, in both

Office and Eucharist, will resume "in course." Except for the major and minor feast days sprinkled throughout these months, there will be no great drama. In other words, the "Time after Pentecost" is like ordinary Christian life. It is time to get on with everyday faithfulness in prayer, study, work, hospitality, and recreation. The agricultural parables Jesus told about the coming kingdom, of its slow but often surprising growth, characterize this time:

> Jesus also said, "The kingdom of God is as if someone would scatter seed on the ground, and would sleep and rise day and night, and the seed would sprout and grow, he does not know how." (Mark 4:26–27)

We go about our daily tasks, sleeping and rising, working and praying, and God gives the growth—often secretly, we "do not know how." And so, our days are sanctified. It happens quietly, day in and day out, year in and year out, through the round of the liturgical year. The sanctification of time transpires through the regular pattern of Daily Office and Eucharist. As we live into these rhythms, we are bought into harmony with cycles of nature, while the mysteries of the Incarnation take flesh in our own.

4 ▪ Learning from Life Together

God sends strangers into the church to mess things up. Strangers don't mean to do this; it's just the way that social systems operate. Strangers come into a known social gathering, one that has learned over time how to operate, what norms are agreeable, and what its relationships mean. Strangers come into these systems more or less ignorant of the way things have always operated in churches. Today, there is no single set of cultural norms related to church that everyone shares. There is no canon of behavior for going to church. If there are norms of behavior in a local congregation, they are less and less understood by first-time church visitors. For some, this is bad news; for others, it is very good news. Strangers come into a social system that insiders understand, and their very presence makes that understanding open to debate. God sends strangers to open the church to a new understanding of its identity. Despite a congregation's best efforts at keeping things the same, strangers bring the disruptive presence of the Spirit with them into the assembly.

Early in my ordained ministry, I was a Canon at Christ Church Cathedral in Houston, Texas. Christ Church is a congregation that has enlivened the heart of that city since 1839. It has outreach programs to aid the homeless, as well as a brilliant liturgy and an exquisite music program. To step into Christ Church is to step into a world where it seems that peace and beauty have always been the order of the day—until it's not. I remember a perfect Sunday morning at Christ Church Cathedral. The sun shone through the stained glass windows, and I stood in the pulpit, preaching the love of God. As I recall, I was talking about Christian responsibility to those in need. I preached from the arrogance and privilege of a newly minted priest. And then it happened. God sent a stranger into our midst. And we all witnessed the coming of Christ.

I didn't know his name; I'd never seen him before. But I knew his type. He was dirty, crazy-eyed, homeless. He was one of the thousands of men who walk the streets and sidewalks and alleys of every American city, muttering angrily under their breath. The people in authority over the cathedral always tried to manage homeless men when they came inside. Not that we would exclude them, the cathedral was a place for everyone. But when a homeless person would walk in, vaguely breathing some threat, the ushers would keep an eye on him.

On this perfect Sunday morning, the homeless stranger walked into the church and quickly up the central aisle, bypassing the ushers and heading straight to the front pew, maybe ten feet in front of the pulpit where I stood. He came to the pew where a friend of mine customarily sat with her family. And he did look dangerously unstable, dangerously unpredictable. He seemed unwilling to be managed by the religious niceties that everyone else either consciously or unconsciously embraced. He waved his hand at my friend, indicating that she had somehow mistakenly taken his regular seat. She moved down the pew a space and let him sit down. An usher, having missed his chance to corral him safely in the back of the cathedral, hurried up the central aisle after him, squatting next to where the man sat. I watched and preached from the high pulpit. God has a wicked sense of humor. When the homeless stranger walked in that morning, I had just hit on the main theme of my sermon: the Christian responsibility to treat homeless people with respect. I did not expect that the invitation to disruption would be taken so literally by God.

I stood, and I preached. Then I looked. And the homeless stranger was crying. His face was wet with tears. Then I looked again. And my friend had wrapped her smooth, manicured hand around his, comforting him as I had seen her comfort her children. At the Peace, I went to my friend and asked, "Is everything okay?" She replied, "Everything is perfect." At communion, she walked hand in hand with her homeless brother to the altar, and I placed the bread of life into his hurt hands. And then he was gone. Like the angel at the empty tomb, his message was given, and he disappeared.

Despite our best efforts, the social system in most congregations will seek to carefully separate people into "us" and "them." We do this because we are afraid. We carry a fear through the church like a wet sofa, fear weighing us down, exhausting us on the way that leads to eternal life. We fear the lack of control that is the very hallmark of Jesus's pathway. We fear the strangeness of the gospel's obvious exhortation: "It is not the healthy who need a doctor, but the sick. I have not come to call the righteous, but sinners." But our fear will not stop the Good News. And this is the Good News: we get to live for the sake of the world, as God truly knows it to be, not just the way we fear it might be. We get to risk embracing strangers with the same embrace God gives. We get to build our future on God's promise to come to us in the presence of the stranger. We get to have the church broken by strangers.

Strangers break open the church and give everyone inside a new experience of God's beauty. Beauty is not only a gift *from* God; it is an experience of God. Beauty is the glory of God, not only a way that we talk about God's glory. Whenever and wherever God is present, there is beauty—including in the presence of strangers. The congregation's work is to welcome strangers with the same wondering desire as we welcome the coming of God's beauty in our midst. But more than that, our responsibility is to welcome the opportunity of transformation that comes in the presence of strangers. In welcoming the stranger, we must expect that we will be remade as a community and as individuals. Welcoming the stranger into our lives must be filled with generosity and void of judgment. We make this choice to welcome strangers because we want to see more of what God is doing in the world and the church.

Since our founding, St. Gregory's has made a preferential choice to welcome strangers into the liturgy without an expectation that they will conform themselves to the congregation's faith or understanding. This insight is based on one of the primary assumptions of our common life: God, who longs to draw the whole world in love, is revealed to the community in the presence of the stranger. Each Sunday we begin our liturgy with this prayer: "Blessed be God the Word, who came to his own and his own received him not; for in this way God glorifies the stranger. O God, show us your image in all who come to us today that we may welcome them and you." Show us! Give to us! We are like the little children that Jesus insists we must become if we are to inherit the Kingdom of God: we want what we want now! We want to see more of God, more of God's action in the world, and we believe that strangers are the ones who are uniquely able to show God to us.

It is God who glorifies strangers, and God's people respond to this divine action by doing the same thing. Glorifying the stranger admits that he or she brings a gift to us: newness, possibility, and potential. This is what makes the stranger beautiful to us. When a stranger comes into the assembly, it is a sign of God's presence, making the whole world new. In response, we go out of our way to welcome them, hoping that, in the encounter, we will discover something that we had not known before about God and God's action in the world. As one member, Randy, says, "I can share myself and whatever joy I have with strangers." Sharing ourselves with strangers begins in our desire to become a friend to the stranger, to know and be known by the stranger. We do this in the context of the liturgy, and we can carry on this practice in our lives outside of the church. Our hope of becoming a friend with another person is beautiful; it is the moment when the stranger ceases being a threat and is revealed as bearing God's image.

Whether or not congregations choose to welcome strangers is the critical question of the day. Until the church understands itself to be peripheral, strange, and outside the dominance culture, it won't be interested in bringing strangers into the center of its life. Perhaps the question for congregations is, "Can we leave our egocentrism and see where God is emerging right now—even if it is strange to us?" The way the church answers this question carries the hope of transforming the world. One of the unique gifts that the church bears for the world is our ability to welcome strangers, as they are. We cannot welcome strangers on the basis of their conformity to our practice. We must welcome them as a sign of God's presence with us, showing us what God is doing in the world, breaking us open to see more of God. Sometimes, we must ourselves become strangers in order to see the work of God in the world.

Being a stranger can be overwhelming. Finding yourself a stranger in the world can make you long nostalgically for the way things were, particularly if you are the sort of person whom the past privileged. Like the Hebrews in the wilderness, we may long for the fleshpots of our captivity. We may want things just to calm down and return to "normal." One Sunday, after a particularly acrimonious conversation with a parishioner, I was slumped over in the sacristy trying to get it together for the next service. Margaret walked in and asked me if I was okay. I said, "Sometimes I just long for the church of the 1950s where everyone did what the rector said." She put her hand on my shoulder and gently replied, "I know. But you'd have been miserable back then."

We cannot return to the past. We cannot go back to a time and place where everyone knew how to behave in church, where people conformed to church ways to be a part of the church. That world has passed away—thanks be to God. As we continue to grow into post-Christendom, as we learn new ways of being the church, we get to embrace our identity as strangers. We get to embrace the truth prophetically uttered by Flannery O'Connor: "You shall know the truth, and the truth shall make you odd." The tendency of human culture is to work hard at creating a world where nothing changes, and if that doesn't work to turn to more violent means of suppression. We who follow the way of Jesus Christ have other options. Instead of violence, we have received a particular intelligence. We are to be like the one the gospel tells us is guarding a house: we have to stay alert, stay awake, and keep patience. We must stay awake to our true identity: we are God's beloved. As God's beloved, we are knit together out of God's desire for us. That is our identity. We are made as God's beloved, the apple of God's eye, and the object of God's desire. This is the identity that we share with every other stranger we encounter. We are, all of us, God's beloved.

By welcoming strangers, and by embracing our own strangeness, we learn more about our own desire to be new, to understand more about God's presence in the world and how we are transformed by it. Randy describes it like this: "I think that we're dancing through history and that we live out the idea of welcoming the stranger. That daily and weekly, that's before us: welcoming the stranger to become God's friend." People at St. Gregory's welcome the stranger, not only as an attempt at social inclusion but to know God. Welcoming the stranger is not just about etiquette; it is a theological and spiritual exercise that expects the beauty of holiness to be revealed in the lives of strangers as God glorifies them.

Mark lives near the Haight-Ashbury neighborhood in San Francisco. Although it was ground zero for the Summer of Love fifty years ago, the neighborhood now swings from being touristy to a layover for homeless people. Like so many of our neighborhoods, it has experienced both the highs and lows of gentrification. Not long ago, the old neighborhood grocery store was turned into a Whole Foods Market. Now it's shared by hipster parents shopping for organic food and homeless men hunting for their next fix. Mark shops there. He told me a story about how he sees God glorifying the stranger at Whole Foods: "For the last six months or so I've realized that there's a particular man. He's very down-and-out. He lives in a sort of group home. He's an older man in a wheelchair that I run into more often than seems to be coincidence. When that started to happen, instead of just sort of thinking, 'Isn't that odd,' I had a different attitude with myself, which was, 'God is putting this man in my path in some way. And I want to engage in that.' And so, whenever I see him, we sit and we talk. I make sure he's had some food that day. Yesterday we had a long talk about his background, and he was telling me how cold he is at night. So the next time I see him, I can give him some blankets."

There is a beguiling social contract that tries to separate Mark from the down-and-out man at Whole Foods. It is the kind of social contract that allows me to look away the instant I might catch a stranger's eye. We get used to this agreement that we make with the stranger and ourselves, to the degree that the stranger stops being a person and becomes a problem. When we dehumanize strangers, we don't have to deal with them, let alone love them. But when our imagination is transformed, when we begin to look at strangers as those who are a part of ourselves, we cannot look away. If we do look away, our consciences remind us that we have been changed. Once you begin to look at the stranger as beautiful, you cannot see them otherwise without diminishing yourself. Mark found that there was a divine intention in a seemingly random encounter with a stranger. Rather than ignore this calling, he chose to pursue it and engage a stranger in conversation, discovering that the neediness of the other was something that he could address himself. Mark saw the man at Whole Foods and was changed by what he saw. His small act of social engagement became an opportunity for transformation. And in all of this he witnessed the magnificence of God who glorifies the stranger.

We glorify the stranger because God glorifies the stranger. To "glorify" means to reveal the essence of a thing. God glorifies the stranger so that we can understand the essential truth of our humanity, that God's love for everyone is the only thing that has the power to relate us to the other. When God glorifies the stranger, we discover our true identity and our vocation in life. We must glorify the stranger as God does. We do this in the ways that we choose to engage those who are strange to us. Looking at the stranger not as a threat, but as a member of God's household, reveals our mutual identity as God's children. As we pay attention to this identity, we learn to know more of God as revealed in Jesus Christ. That learning isn't an intellectual exercise; it is about love.

Jesus is glorified as he is lifted high upon the cross, drawing all people into his embrace. This is the one thing that he can do to reveal perfectly the essence of God. On the hard wood of the cross, Jesus glorifies God as the one who is absolute, sacrificial love. Jesus reveals what God's love is like by saying, "Look, I'm dying for you—and I'm doing it freely and in full control of the situation. Don't worry about how you will know me—I've known you perfectly by becoming perfectly like you—even bleeding and dying like you." This is God's love in action. God joins in solidarity with us, showing the fullness of love. There is no place that God has not gone before us because Jesus has revealed God to us perfectly. So, when Jesus weeps, God weeps. When Jesus bleeds, God bleeds. When Jesus dies, God dies. When Jesus rises to new life, God promises to rise up in us anew.

Jesus gives us a way to become visible to the world around us. For the world to be able to see him, Jesus gives his followers a new commandment: "Love one another." The promise is that whenever we love, the world will see what Jesus is like and if the world sees what Jesus is like, then the world will see what God is like. Not because we are perfect, but because we were first loved into life by God. Everyone will be able to see God because God first loved us. As we enact the love God gives us, we are glorified, and we glorify the stranger.

To be transformed in its shared life, congregations have to welcome everyone into the community irrespective of belief, differences, or familiarity. Welcoming strangers, without requiring them to know everything about our congregational culture, is transformative. It's this kind of generous welcome that places the experience of the stranger at the center of the community's imagination. Designing the liturgy, formation, community life, and service in ways that speak clearly to strangers is something that any congregation in the Episcopal Church can do. The congregation's need for welcoming strangers must be expressed as part of its own culture and practice.

We must learn to structure our shared life to show that God is reaching out to all beings, calling everyone into friendship. There can be no distinctions; God has already established all of us as beloved friends. As God's friends, we are being made new. In Paul's Epistle to the Colossians the writer says, "You have stripped off the old self with its practices and have clothed yourselves with the new self, which is being renewed in knowledge according to the image of its creator. In that renewal there is no longer Greek and Jew, circumcised and uncircumcised, barbarian, Scythian, slave and free; but Christ is all and in all" (Colossians 3:9b–11). God in Christ is making the church anew, breaking down divisions, and calling us to renewal of life. Our renewal as God's people means that we cannot define ourselves against those who are strangers. We are called to see Christ in all people, living in God's friendship.

God is at work breaking down the divisions that deform our relationships. God is at work in what is strange to us and in us. We must engage the unknown world where God is to be found. We are transformed whenever we recognize God's presence in our experiences, relationships, and efforts at creating what has not yet been known. In all of this, we strive to grow into the image of the Creator, to whom no one is a stranger. Friendship with God, established by the loving service of Jesus Christ to all humanity, remakes the church's identity as a community of friends, each striving to do the work of Christ in the world.

TURN: Pause, listen, and choose to follow Jesus

THE WAY OF LOVE

*As Jesus was walking along, he saw Levi son of
 Alphaeus sitting at the tax booth, and he said to
 him, "Follow me." And he got up and followed him.
 – Mark 2:14*

*"Do you turn to Jesus Christ . . . ?"
 – Book of Common Prayer, 302*

Like the disciples, we are called by Jesus to follow the Way
of Love. With God's help, we can turn from the powers of
sin, hatred, fear, injustice, and oppression toward the
way of truth, love, hope, justice, and freedom. In turning,
we reorient our lives to Jesus Christ, falling in love again, again, and again.

For Reflection and Discernment

- What practices help you to turn again and again to Jesus and the Way
  of Love?
- How will (or do) you incorporate these practices into your rhythm of life?
- Who will be your companion as you turn toward Jesus?

LEARN: Reflect on Scripture each day, especially on Jesus's life and teachings.

*"Those who love me will keep my word, and my Father will love them,
 and we will come to them and make our home with them." – John 14:23*

*Grant us so to hear [the Holy Scriptures], read, mark, learn, and inwardly
 digest them. – Book of Common Prayer, 236*

By reading and reflecting on Scripture, especially the life and teachings of
Jesus, we draw near to God, and God's word dwells in us. When we open our
minds and hearts to Scripture, we learn to see God's story and God's activity
in everyday life.

For Reflection and Discernment

- What ways of reflecting on Scripture are most life-giving for you?
- When will you set aside time to read and reflect on Scripture in your day?
- With whom will you share in the commitment to read and reflect on
  Scripture?

PRAY: Dwell intentionally with God daily

He was praying in a certain place, and after he had finished,
  one of his disciples said to him, "Lord, teach us to pray,
  as John taught his disciples." – Luke 11:1

"Lord, hear our prayer." – Book of Common Prayer

Jesus teaches us to come before God with humble hearts, boldly offering our
thanksgivings and concerns to God or simply listening for God's voice in our
lives and in the world. Whether in thought, word, or deed, individually or
corporately, when we pray we invite and dwell in God's loving presence.

For Reflection and Discernment

- What intentional prayer practices center you in God's presence, so
  you can hear, speak, or simply dwell with God?
- How will (or do) you incorporate intentional prayer into your daily life?
- With whom will you share in the commitment to pray?

WORSHIP: Gather in community weekly to thank, praise, and dwell with God

When he was at the table with them, he took bread, blessed and broke it,
  and gave it to them. Then their eyes were opened, and they recognized him.
  – Luke 24:30-31

Celebrant: Lift up your hearts. People: We lift them to the Lord.
  – Book of Common Prayer, 361

When we worship, we gather with others before God. We hear the Good
News of Jesus, give thanks, confess, and offer the brokenness of the world to
God. As we break bread, our eyes are opened to the presence of Christ. By the
power of the Holy Spirit, we are made one body, the body of Christ sent forth
to live the Way of Love.

For Discernment and Reflection

- What communal worship practices move you to encounter God and
  knit you into the body of Christ?
- How will (or do) you commit to regularly worship?
- With whom will you share the commitment to worship this week?

BLESS: Share faith and unselfishly give and serve

"Freely you have received; freely give." – Matthew 10:8

Celebrant: Will you proclaim by word and example the Good News of God in Christ?
People: We will, with God's help. – Book of Common Prayer, 305

Jesus called his disciples to give, forgive, teach, and heal in his name. We are empowered by the Spirit to bless everyone we meet, practicing generosity and compassion and proclaiming the Good News of God in Christ with hopeful words and selfless actions. We can share our stories of blessing and invite others to the Way of Love.

For Discernment and Reflection

- What are the ways the Spirit is calling you to bless others?
- How will (or does) blessing others through sharing your resources, faith, and story become part of your daily life?
- Who will join you in committing to the practice of blessing others

GO: Cross boundaries, listen deeply, and live like Jesus

Jesus said to them, "Peace be with you. As the Father has sent me,
  so I send you." – John 20:21

Send them into the world in witness to your love.
  – Book of Common Prayer, 306

As Jesus went to the highways and byways, he sends us beyond our circles and comfort to witness to the love, justice, and truth of God with our lips and with our lives. We go to listen with humility and to join God in healing a hurting world. We go to become Beloved Community, a people reconciled in love with God and one another.

For Discernment and Reflection

- To what new places or communities is the Spirit sending you to witness to the love, justice, and truth of God?
- How will you build into your life a commitment to cross boundaries, listen carefully, and take part in healing and reconciling what is broken in this world?
- With whom will you share in the commitment to go forth as a reconciler and healer?

REST: Receive the gift of God's grace, peace, and restoration

Peace I leave with you; my peace I give you. I do not give to you
  as the world gives. Do not let your hearts be troubled
  and do not be afraid. – John 14:27

Blessed are you, O Lord . . . giving rest to the weary,
  renewing the strength of those who are spent.
  – Book of Common Prayer, 113

From the beginning of creation, god has established the sacred pattern of going and returning, labor and rest. Especially today, God invites us to dedicate time for restoration and wholeness—within our bodies, minds, and souls, and within our communities and institutions. By resting, we place our trust in God; the primary actor who brings all things to their fullness.

For Discernment and Reflection

- What practices restore your body, mind and soul?
- How will you observe rest and renewal on a regular basis?
- With whom will you commit to create and maintain a regular practice of rest?

CPSIA information can be obtained
at www.ICGtesting.com
Printed in the USA
LVHW031710201019
634697LV00003B/3/P

9 781640 651708